OUR LADY

V. Pray for us, O holy Mother of God,
R. *That we may be made worthy of the promises of Christ.*

THE BLESSED VIRGIN MARY
MOTHER OF GOD
AT THE ANNUNCIATION.
HAIL MARY, FULL OF GRACE!

FAVORITE PRAYERS TO
OUR LADY

Compiled from Traditional Sources

"Hail, full of grace,
the Lord is with thee: blessed
art thou among women."
(*Luke* 1:28)

TAN Books
Charlotte, North Carolina

Illustrations: Pages ii, 13-27, 40, 43, drawn by Gabrielle M. Hall (many based on line drawings by Philip Schumacher in *Bible History* by Schuster) and copyright © 2010 by TAN Books, except pp. 14 and 40 copyright © 2007 by TAN Books and p. 15 copyright © 2005 by TAN Books. Page 30, copyright © 2001 by TAN Books. Pages 33, 50-53, Janssens; pp. 36, 39, 54, *Le Catechisme en images*; p. 37, photo: Queen of the Americas Guild, St. Charles, IL; p. 38, Philip Schumacher (from *Bible History* by Schuster); p. 58, painting by Heinrich Kaiser (1813-1900), photo by Victoria Ambrosetti, photo copyright © 2005 by TAN Books.

Cover design by Sebrina Higdon.

Cover photo: Stained glass image of Our Lady of Lourdes, Dominican Priory, London. Brother Lawrence Lew, O.P.

ISBN 978-0-89555-901-2

Printed and bound in the United States of America.

TAN Books
Charlotte, North Carolina
2010

MAGNIFICAT

"MY SOUL doth magnify the Lord, and my spirit hath rejoiced in God my Saviour, because He hath regarded the humility of His handmaid: for behold, from henceforth all generations shall call me blessed, because He that is mighty hath done great things to me, and holy is His Name. And His mercy is from generation unto generations, to them that fear Him.

"He hath showed might in His arm: He hath scattered the proud in the conceit of their heart. He hath put down the mighty from their seat, and hath exalted the humble. He hath filled the hungry with good things, and the rich He hath sent empty away. He hath received Israel His servant, being mindful of His mercy: as He spoke to our fathers, to Abraham and to his seed forever."

—*The Blessed Virgin Mary*
Luke 1:46-55

FAVORITE
PRAYERS TO
OUR LADY

HAIL MARY
The Angelic Salutation

HAIL MARY, full of grace, the Lord is with thee; blessed art thou among women, and blessed is the Fruit of thy womb, Jesus. Holy Mary, Mother of God, pray for us sinners, now and at the hour of our death. Amen.

HAIL HOLY QUEEN
Salve Regina

HAIL HOLY QUEEN, Mother of mercy, our life, our sweetness and our hope! To thee do we cry, poor banished children of Eve. To thee do we send up our sighs, mourning and weeping in this valley of tears. Turn then, most gracious advocate, thine eyes of mercy toward us. And after this our exile, show unto us the blessed Fruit of thy womb, Jesus. O clement, O loving, O sweet Virgin Mary.

V. Pray for us, O holy Mother of God,
R. *That we may be made worthy of the promises of Christ.*

MEMORARE
By St. Bernard of Clairvaux (d. 1153)

REMEMBER, O most gracious Virgin Mary, that never was it known that anyone who fled to thy protection, implored thy help or sought thy intercession was left unaided. Inspired with this confidence, I fly unto thee, O Virgin of virgins, my Mother. To thee do I come, before thee I stand, sinful and sorrowful. O Mother of the Word Incarnate, despise not my petitions, but in thy mercy hear and answer me. Amen.

THE THREE HAIL MARYS

This devotion, highly recommended by saints, consists of reciting the Hail Mary three times morning and evening every day of one's life, followed by this aspiration: "O Mother mine, keep me from mortal sin this day (night); O Mother mine, keep me from mortal sin forever." The Hail Marys are recited in honor of Our Lady's Immaculate Conception.

The practice of the Three Hail Marys is especially recommended for obtaining the virtue of purity.

THE SEVEN JOYS OF MARY
As listed in the Franciscan Crown. Other versions include the Ascension and the Descent of the Holy Ghost.

1. The Annunciation
2. The Visitation
3. The Nativity
4. The Adoration by the Magi
5. The Finding of Our Lord in the Temple
6. The Resurrection
7. The Assumption and Coronation of Our Lady

THE ANGELUS

The Angelus is traditionally prayed standing, in the morning (6:00 a.m.), at noon and in the evening (6:00 p.m.), throughout the year, except during Paschal Time (Easter Sunday through the evening of the Saturday preceding Trinity Sunday), when the Regina Coeli is prayed instead.

V. The Angel of the Lord declared unto Mary.
R. *And she conceived of the Holy Ghost.*
   Hail Mary . . .

V. Behold the handmaid of the Lord.
R. *Be it done unto me according to thy word.*
   Hail Mary . . .

V. And the Word was made Flesh. *(Genuflect.)*
R. *And dwelt among us. (Arise.)*
   Hail Mary . . .

V. Pray for us, O holy Mother of God,
R. *That we may be made worthy of the promises of Christ.*

Let Us Pray

Pour forth, we beseech Thee, O Lord, Thy grace into our hearts, that we to whom the Incarnation of Christ, Thy Son, was made known by the message of an angel, may by His Passion and Cross be brought to the glory of His Resurrection. Through the same Christ Our Lord. Amen.

REGINA COELI

This prayer is traditionally prayed standing, in the morning (6:00 a.m.), at noon and in the evening (6:00 p.m.) during Paschal Time (from Easter Sunday through the evening of the Saturday preceding Trinity Sunday) instead of The Angelus.

V. Queen of Heaven, rejoice. Alleluia.
R. *For He whom thou wast worthy to bear. Alleluia.*

V. Has risen as He said. Alleluia.
R. *Pray for us to God. Alleluia.*

V. Rejoice and be glad, O Virgin Mary. Alleluia.
R. *For the Lord is truly risen. Alleluia.*

Let Us Pray

O God, Who by the Resurrection of Thy Son, Our Lord Jesus Christ, hast been pleased to give joy to the whole world, grant, we beseech Thee, that through the intercession of the Virgin Mary, His Mother, we may attain the joys of eternal life. Through the same Christ Our Lord. Amen.

WORDS OF ST. LOUIS DE MONTFORT

"Both St. Bernard and St. Bonaventure say that the Queen of Heaven is certainly no less grateful and conscientious than gracious and well-mannered people of this world. Just as she excels in all other perfections, she surpasses us all in the virtue of gratitude; so she would never let us honor her with love and respect without repaying us one hundredfold. St. Bonaventure says that Mary will greet us with grace if we greet her with the Hail Mary." (*Secret of the Rosary*, p. 47).

WORDS OF THE ARCHANGEL GABRIEL TO OUR LADY

"Hail, full of grace, the Lord is with thee: blessed art thou among women. . . . Behold thou shalt conceive in thy womb, and shalt bring forth a Son; and thou shalt call His name Jesus. He shall be great, and shall be called the Son of the Most High, and the Lord God shall give unto Him the throne of David His father: and He shall reign in the house of Jacob for ever, and of His kingdom there shall be no end."—*Luke* 1:28-33

JESUS, MARY AND JOSEPH

JESUS, Mary and Joseph, I give thee my heart and my soul.

Jesus, Mary and Joseph, assist me in my last agony.

Jesus, Mary and Joseph, may I breathe forth my soul in peace with thee.

WE FLY TO THY PATRONAGE
(Sub Tuum Praesidium)

WE fly to thy patronage, O holy Mother of God. Despise not our petitions in our necessities, but deliver us always from all dangers, O glorious and blessed Virgin.

WORDS OF ST. METHODIUS (d. 847)

"By the prayers of Mary, almost innumerable sinners are converted."

HOW TO PRAY THE ROSARY

1. Make the *Sign of the Cross* and say *The Apostles' Creed.*
2. Say the *Our Father.*
3. Say 3 *Hail Marys.*
4. Say the *Glory Be to the Father.*
5. Announce the First Mystery; then say the *Our Father.*
6. Say 10 *Hail Marys.*
7. Say the *Glory Be to the Father.*
8. Say the *O My Jesus.*
9. Announce the Second Mystery; then say the *Our Father,* 10 *Hail Marys, Glory Be* and *O My Jesus.*
10. Announce the Third Mystery; then say the *Our Father,* 10 *Hail Marys, Glory Be* and *O My Jesus.*
11. Announce the Fourth Mystery; then say the *Our Father,* 10 *Hail Marys, Glory Be* and *O My Jesus.*
12. Announce the Fifth Mystery; then say the *Our Father,*

10 *Hail Marys, Glory Be* and *O My Jesus.*

13. Conclude by saying the *Hail, Holy Queen.*

14. Follow with *Prayer after the Rosary,* if desired.

THE MYSTERIES OF THE ROSARY

(The classic 15 Mysteries of Our Lady of Fatima.)
To be meditated upon while praying the Rosary.

THE JOYFUL MYSTERIES
Said on Mondays and Thursdays and the Sundays from the First Sunday of Advent until Lent.

1st Joyful Mystery: The Annunciation
2nd Joyful Mystery: The Visitation
3rd Joyful Mystery: The Nativity
4th Joyful Mystery: The Presentation of Our Lord in the Temple
5th Joyful Mystery: The Finding of Our Lord in the Temple

THE SORROWFUL MYSTERIES
Said on Tuesdays and Fridays and the Sundays of Lent.

1st Sorrowful Mystery: The Agony in the Garden
2nd Sorrowful Mystery: The Scourging at the Pillar
3rd Sorrowful Mystery: The Crowning with Thorns
4th Sorrowful Mystery: The Carrying of the Cross
5th Sorrowful Mystery: The Crucifixion and Death of Our Lord on the Cross

THE GLORIOUS MYSTERIES
Said on Wednesdays and Saturdays and the Sundays from Easter until Advent.

1st Glorious Mystery: The Resurrection of Our Lord
2nd Glorious Mystery: The Ascension of Our Lord
3rd Glorious Mystery: The Descent of the Holy Ghost upon the Apostles

4th Glorious Mystery: The Assumption of the Blessed
Virgin Mary into Heaven
5th Glorious Mystery: The Coronation of Our Lady as
Queen of Heaven and Earth

THE LUMINOUS MYSTERIES *

1st Luminous Mystery: The Baptism in the Jordan
2nd Luminous Mystery: Our Lord's Self-manifestation
at the Wedding of Cana
3rd Luminous Mystery: The proclamation of the
Kingdom of God and call to
conversion
4th Luminous Mystery: The Transfiguration
5th Luminous Mystery: The Institution of the Eucharist,
as the sacramental expression
of the Paschal Mystery

* *The Luminous Mysteries were suggested by Pope John Paul II in 2002 as an optional addition to the traditional 15-decade Rosary. He suggested that the Luminous Mysteries be said on Thursdays, with Saturday being changed to a day for praying the Joyful Mysteries.*

PRAYERS OF THE ROSARY

The Sign of the Cross

IN THE NAME of the Father, and of the Son, and of the Holy Ghost. Amen.

The Apostles' Creed

I BELIEVE in God, the Father Almighty, Creator of heaven and earth; and in Jesus Christ, His only Son, Our Lord; who was conceived by the Holy Ghost, born of the Virgin Mary, suffered under

Pontius Pilate, was crucified, died, and was buried. He descended into hell; the third day He arose again from the dead; He ascended into Heaven, sitteth at the right hand of God, the Father Almighty; from thence He shall come to judge the living and the dead. I believe in the Holy Ghost, the Holy Catholic Church, the Communion of Saints, the forgiveness of sins, the resurrection of the body, and life everlasting. Amen.

Our Father

OUR FATHER, Who art in Heaven, hallowed be Thy Name. Thy kingdom come, Thy will be done on earth as it is in Heaven. Give us this day our daily bread, and forgive us our trespasses, as we forgive those who trespass against us. And lead us not into temptation, but deliver us from evil. Amen.

Hail Mary

HAIL MARY, full of grace, the Lord is with thee; blessed art thou among women, and blessed is the Fruit of thy womb, Jesus. Holy Mary, Mother of God, pray for us sinners, now and at the hour of our death. Amen.

Glory Be

GLORY BE to the Father, and to the Son, and to the Holy Ghost. As it was in the beginning, is now, and ever shall be, world without end. Amen.

O My Jesus

To be said after the Glory Be following each decade of the Rosary.

O MY JESUS, forgive us our sins, save us from the fires of Hell; lead all souls to Heaven, especially those who are most in need of Thy mercy.

Hail Holy Queen
Salve Regina

HAIL HOLY QUEEN, Mother of mercy, our life, our sweetness and our hope! To thee do we cry, poor banished children of Eve. To thee do we send up our sighs, mourning and weeping in this valley of tears. Turn then, most gracious advocate, thine eyes of mercy toward us. And after this our exile, show unto us the blessed Fruit of thy womb, Jesus. O clement, O loving, O sweet Virgin Mary.

V. Pray for us, O holy Mother of God,
R. *That we may be made worthy of the promises of Christ.*

Prayer after the Rosary

O GOD, Whose only-begotten Son, by His life, death and Resurrection, has purchased for us the rewards of eternal salvation, grant, we beseech Thee, that, meditating upon these Mysteries of the Most Holy Rosary of the Blessed Virgin Mary, we may both imitate what they contain and obtain what they promise. Through the same Christ Our Lord. Amen.

THE FIVE FIRST SATURDAYS

On July 13, 1917 Our Lady of Fatima said, "I shall come to ask for . . . the Communion of Reparation on the First Saturdays."

Our Lady fulfilled this promise when she and the Child Jesus appeared to Sister Lucia on December 10, 1925. Our Lady said:

"Look, my daughter, at my heart, surrounded by thorns with which ungrateful men pierce me at every moment by their blasphemies and ingratitude. You, at least, try to console me, and announce in my name that I promise to assist at the hour of death, with all the graces necessary for salvation, all those who, on the first Saturday of five consecutive months, confess, receive Holy Communion, recite five decades of the Rosary and keep me company for fifteen minutes meditating on the fifteen mysteries of the Rosary, with the intention of making reparation to me."

On another occasion, Our Lord appeared to Sister

Lucia and told her that the Confession could be made within eight days of the First Saturday, or even later on, provided that one were in the state of grace when receiving Communion and had the intention of making reparation to the Immaculate Heart of Mary. Regarding those who forget to form this intention, Our Lord answered: "They can form it at the next Confession, taking advantage of their first opportunity to go to Confession."

The 15-minute meditation does not have to cover all 15 Mysteries. Sister Lucia explained that she herself meditated on only one Mystery each First Saturday, going through the 15 Mysteries one by one and then beginning again with the Annunciation.

MEDITATIONS ON THE 15 MYSTERIES OF THE ROSARY

Requested by Our Lady of Fatima as part of the First Saturday Devotion.

The following pages may be used for making the First Saturday meditations or for praying the Rosary at any time. The meditations are those of St. Louis De Montfort.

Whether praying the Rosary or making the First Saturday meditations, one need not read through all ten points for each Mystery. One or two might provide ample food for mind and heart.

THE FIVE JOYFUL MYSTERIES

1. The Annunciation

We offer Thee, O Lord Jesus, this first decade in honor of Thy Incarnation in Mary's womb; and we ask of Thee, through this Mystery and through her intercession, a profound humility. Amen.

OUR FATHER. Charity of God: Immense.

TEN HAIL MARYS.

1. To deplore the unhappy state of the disobedient Adam; his own just condemnation, as well as that of all his children.
2. To honor the desires of the Patriarchs and Prophets who longed for the Messias.
3. To honor the wishes and prayers of the Blessed Virgin for the speedy coming of the Messias, and to honor her marriage with St. Joseph.
4. To honor the charity of the Eternal Father, who gave up His Son.
5. To honor the love of the Son, who delivered Himself up for us.
6. To honor the mission and the salutation of the Angel Gabriel.
7. To honor the virginal fear of Mary.
8. To honor the faith and the consent of Mary.
9. To honor the creation of the soul and the formation of the body of Jesus Christ in the womb of Mary, by the operation of the Holy Spirit.
10. To honor the adoration by the Angels of the Word Incarnate in the womb of Mary.

May the grace of the Mystery of the Annunciation come down into our souls. Amen.

2. The Visitation

We offer Thee, O Lord Jesus, this second decade in honor of the Visitation of Thy holy Mother to her cousin St. Elizabeth and the sanctification of St. John the Baptist; and we ask of Thee, through this Mystery and through the intercession of Thy holy Mother, charity toward our neighbor. Amen.

OUR FATHER. Majesty of God: Adorable.

TEN HAIL MARYS.

1. To honor the joy of the heart of Mary in the possession of Jesus.
2. To honor the sacrifice that Jesus Christ made of Himself to His Eternal Father by coming into this world.
3. To honor the love that Jesus and Mary had for each other.
4. To recall St. Joseph's doubts concerning Mary's pregnancy.
5. To honor the choice of the Elect, planned by Jesus and Mary.
6. To honor the fervor of Mary in her visit to her cousin St. Elizabeth.
7. To honor the salutation of Mary and the sanctification of St. John the Baptist and of his mother, St. Elizabeth.
8. To honor the gratitude of the Blessed Virgin toward God in the Magnificat.
9. To honor her charity and humility in serving her cousin.
10. To honor the mutual dependence of Jesus and Mary and that which we should have in regard to them.

May the grace of the Mystery of the Visitation come down into our souls. Amen.

3. The Nativity

We offer Thee, O Lord Jesus, this third decade in honor of Thy Nativity in the stable of Bethlehem; and we ask of Thee, through this Mystery and through the intercession of Thy holy Mother, detachment from the things of the world, contempt of riches and love of poverty. Amen.

OUR FATHER. Riches of God: Infinite.

TEN HAIL MARYS.

1. To honor Mary and Joseph in the contempt and rejection they suffered in Bethlehem.
2. To honor the poverty of the stable in which God was born.
3. To honor the deep contemplation and the immense love of Mary.
4. To honor the virginal birth of Jesus.
5. To honor the adoration and the canticles of the Angels at the birth of Jesus Christ.
6. To honor the enchanting beauty of His divine infancy.
7. To honor the coming of the shepherds, bringing their gifts to the stable.
8. To honor the circumcision of Jesus.
9. To honor the imposition of the name of Jesus and its grandeur.
10. To honor the adoration of the Magi Kings and their presents.

May the grace of the Mystery of the Nativity come down into our souls. Amen.

4. The Presentation in
the Temple

We offer Thee, O Lord Jesus, this fourth decade in honor of Thy Presentation in the Temple and the Purification of Mary; and we ask of Thee, through this Mystery and through the intercession of Thy holy Mother, great purity of body and soul. Amen.

OUR FATHER. Wisdom of God: Eternal.

TEN HAIL MARYS.

1. To honor the obedience of Jesus and Mary to the Law.
2. To honor the sacrifice that Jesus made of His humanity.
3. To honor the sacrifice that Mary made of her reputation.
4. To honor the joy and the canticles of Simeon and of Anna, the Prophetess.
5. To honor the ransoming of Jesus Christ through the offering of two turtle doves.
6. To recall the massacre of the Holy Innocents by the cruelty of Herod.
7. To honor the flight of Jesus Christ to Egypt, and the obedience of St. Joseph to the voice of the Angel.
8. To honor Our Lord's mysterious stay in Egypt.
9. To honor His return to Nazareth.
10. To honor His growing in age and wisdom.

May the grace of the Mystery of the Presentation in the Temple come down into our souls. Amen.

5. The Finding of Our Lord
in the Temple

We offer Thee, O Lord Jesus, this fifth decade in honor of Mary's finding Thee in the Temple; and we ask of Thee, through this Mystery and through her intercession, the gift of true wisdom. Amen.

OUR FATHER. Sanctity of God: Incomprehensible.
TEN HAIL MARYS.

1. To honor Our Lord's hidden life, laborious and obedient in His home at Nazareth.
2. To honor His preaching and His being found in the Temple among the doctors.
3. To honor His baptism by St. John the Baptist.
4. To honor His fast and temptation in the desert.
5. To honor His admirable preaching.
6. To honor His astonishing miracles.
7. To honor the choice of His twelve Apostles and the powers He gives them.
8. To honor His marvelous Transfiguration.
9. To honor the washing of the feet of the Apostles.
10. To honor the institution of the Holy Eucharist.

May the grace of the Mystery of the Finding of Our Lord in the Temple come down into our souls. Amen.

THE FIVE SORROWFUL MYSTERIES

1. The Agony in the Garden

We offer Thee, O Lord Jesus, this sixth decade in honor of Thy Agony in the Garden of Olives; and we ask of Thee, through this Mystery and through the intercession of Thy holy Mother, contrition for our sins. Amen.

OUR FATHER. Happiness of God: Essential.

TEN HAIL MARYS.

1. To honor the divine retreats made by Our Lord during His life, especially in the garden of agony.
2. To honor the humble, fervent prayers offered by Our Lord during His life and on the eve of His Passion.
3. To honor the patience and kindness with which He treated His Apostles, especially in the Garden.
4. To honor the loneliness of His soul during His whole life, especially in the Garden of Olives.
5. To honor the streams of blood into which anguish plunged Him.
6. To honor the consolation He greatly desired from an angel.
7. To honor His conformity to the Will of His Father, despite the repugnance of nature.
8. To honor the courage with which He approached His executioners, and the force of speech by which He threw them down and then raised them up again.
9. His betrayal by Judas and His captivity by the Jews.
10. His abandonment by His Apostles.

May the grace of the Mystery of the Agony in the Garden come down into our souls. Amen.

2. The Scourging at the Pillar

We offer Thee, O Lord Jesus, this seventh decade in honor of Thy bloody scourging; and we ask of Thee, through this Mystery and through the intercession of Thy holy Mother, the grace of mortifying our senses. Amen.

OUR FATHER. Patience of God: Admirable.

TEN HAIL MARYS.

1. To honor Christ as He is bound with the chains and cords.
2. To honor Christ as He is slapped in the face.
3. To honor Christ in the denials of St. Peter.
4. To honor Christ in the ignominies which He received at Herod's court, when He was clothed with a white robe.
5. To honor Christ in the stripping of His clothes.
6. To honor Christ for the contempt and insults He received from the executioners.
7. To honor Christ beaten and torn by the knotty rods and the cruel whips.
8. To honor the column to which He was tied.
9. To honor the blood which He shed and the wounds He received.
10. To honor His collapse in His own blood.

May the grace of the Mystery of the Scourging at the Pillar come down into our souls. Amen.

3. The Crowning
with Thorns

We offer Thee, O Lord Jesus, this eighth decade in honor of Thy being crowned with thorns; and we ask of Thee, through this Mystery and through the intercession of Thy holy Mother, contempt of the world. Amen.

OUR FATHER. Beauty of God: Unspeakable.

TEN HAIL MARYS.

1. To honor Christ being stripped for the third time.
2. To honor His crown of thorns.
3. To honor the veil with which they bound His eyes.
4. To honor Christ for the blows and spit with which they covered His face.
5. To honor the old cloak which they placed upon His shoulders.
6. To honor the reed which they placed in His hands.
7. To honor the column stump upon which He was placed.
8. To honor Christ for the outrages and insults offered Him.
9. To honor Christ for the blows which He received upon His adorable head.
10. To honor Christ for the derision of which He was the object.

May the grace of the Mystery of the Crowning with Thorns come down into our souls. Amen.

4. The Carrying of
the Cross

We offer Thee, O Lord Jesus, this ninth decade in honor of Thy carrying of the Cross; and we ask of Thee, through this Mystery and through the intercession of Thy holy Mother, patience in bearing our crosses. Amen.

OUR FATHER. The Omnipotence of God: Boundless.

TEN HAIL MARYS.

1. To honor Our Lord's presentation before the populace, the *"Ecce Homo."*
2. To honor Our Lord for the insult of the preference of Barabbas to His Person.
3. To honor Our Lord as the false witnesses testify against Him.
4. To honor Our Lord in His condemnation to death.
5. To honor the love with which He embraced and kissed His cross.
6. To honor the tremendous pains He suffered in carrying it.
7. To honor His falls, due to weakness, beneath His burden.
8. To honor the sorrowful meeting with His holy Mother.
9. To honor the veil of Veronica, upon which His features were imprinted.
10. To honor His tears, those of His holy Mother, and of the holy women who followed Him to Calvary.

May the grace of the Mystery of the Carrying of the Cross come down into our souls. Amen.

5. The Crucifixion

We offer Thee, O Lord Jesus, this tenth decade in honor of Thy Crucifixion and ignominious death on Calvary; and we ask of Thee, through this Mystery and through the intercession of Thy holy Mother, the conversion of sinners, the perseverance of the just, and the relief of the souls in Purgatory. Amen.

OUR FATHER. Justice of God: Tremendous.

TEN HAIL MARYS.

1. To honor the five wounds of Our Lord and His blood shed upon the Cross.
2. To honor His pierced Heart and the Cross upon which He was crucified.
3. To honor the nails and the spear that pierced Him, the sponge and the gall and also the vinegar which He was given to drink.
4. To honor Christ for the shame and infamy which He suffered in being crucified between two thieves.
5. To honor the compassion of His holy Mother.
6. To honor His seven last words.
7. To honor His abandonment and silence.
8. To honor the distress of the whole universe.
9. To honor His cruel and ignominious death.
10. To honor His descent from the Cross and His burial.

May the grace of the Mystery of the Crucifixion come down into our souls. Amen.

THE FIVE GLORIOUS MYSTERIES

1. The Resurrection

We offer Thee, O Lord Jesus, this eleventh decade in honor of Thy glorious Resurrection; and we ask of Thee, through this Mystery and through the intercession of Thy holy Mother, love of God and fervor in Thy service. Amen.

OUR FATHER. Eternity of God: Without beginning.

TEN HAIL MARYS.

1. To honor the descent of Our Lord's soul into Limbo.
2. To honor the joy and the release of the souls of the ancient Fathers who were in Limbo.
3. To honor the reunion of Our Lord's soul to His body in His sepulchre.
4. To honor His miraculous departure from His sepulchre.
5. To honor His victory over death and sin, the world and the devil.
6. To honor the four glorious qualities of His body.
7. To honor the power which He received from His Father in Heaven and on earth.
8. To honor the apparitions with which He honored His holy Mother, His Apostles and His disciples.
9. To honor the communications He had with Heaven and the meal He had with His disciples.
10. To honor the authority and the mission which He gave them to go and preach throughout the whole world.

May the grace of the Mystery of the Resurrection come down into our souls. Amen.

2. The Ascension

We offer Thee, O Lord Jesus, this twelfth decade in honor of Thy triumphant Ascension; and we ask of Thee, through this Mystery and through the intercession of Thy holy Mother, an ardent desire for Heaven, our true home. Amen.

OUR FATHER. The Immensity of God: Limitless.
TEN HAIL MARYS.

1. To honor the promise that Christ would send the Holy Spirit.
2. To honor the reunion of all His disciples upon the Mount of Olives.
3. To honor the blessing which He gave them as He ascended into Heaven.
4. To honor Our Lord's glorious Ascension into Heaven, by His own proper power.
5. To honor the divine welcome and triumph which He received from God His Father and from the entire celestial court.
6. To honor the triumphant powers with which He opened the gates of Heaven.
7. To honor Our Lord's sitting at the right of His Father, equal to Him.
8. To honor the power which He received to judge the living and the dead.
9. To honor His last coming upon earth, when His power and majesty will shine forth in all its splendor.
10. To honor the justice which He will exercise at the Last Judgment, recompensing the good and punishing the wicked for all eternity.

May the grace of the Mystery of the Ascension come down into our souls. Amen.

3. The Descent of the Holy Spirit

We offer Thee, O Lord Jesus, this thirteenth decade in honor of the Mystery of Pentecost; and we ask of Thee, through this Mystery and through the intercession of Thy holy Mother, the coming of the Holy Spirit into our souls. Amen.

OUR FATHER. Providence of God: Universal.

TEN HAIL MARYS.

1. To honor the truth of the Holy Spirit, God, who proceeds from the Father and the Son.
2. To honor the sending of the Holy Spirit to the Apostles.
3. To honor the great noise with which He descended, a sign of His force and power.
4. To honor the tongues of fire sent upon the Apostles to give them the knowledge of Scripture and the love of God and their neighbor.
5. To honor the plenitude of graces with which the Holy Spirit privileged Mary, His faithful spouse.
6. To honor His marvelous conduct toward all the Saints, and toward the very person of Jesus Christ, whom He conducted during His whole life.
7. To honor the Twelve Fruits of the Holy Spirit.
8. To honor the Seven Gifts of the Holy Spirit.
9. To ask for the gift of Wisdom and the coming of His reign in the hearts of men.
10. To obtain victory over the three evil spirits: the flesh, the world and the devil.

May the grace of the Mystery of Pentecost come down into our souls. Amen.

4. The Assumption

We offer Thee, O Lord Jesus, this fourteenth decade in honor of the resurrection and triumphant Assumption of Thy holy Mother into Heaven; and we ask of Thee, through this Mystery and through her intercession, a tender devotion for so good a Mother. Amen.

OUR FATHER. Liberality of God: Unspeakable.

TEN HAIL MARYS.

1. To honor the eternal predestination of Mary as the masterpiece of God's hands.
2. To honor her Immaculate Conception and the fullness of grace and reason in the womb of her mother, St. Anne.
3. To honor her nativity, which has gladdened the world.
4. To honor her presentation and her stay in the Temple.
5. To honor her admirable life, exempt from all sin.
6. To honor the plenitude of her singular virtues.
7. To honor her fruitful virginity and painless childbirth.
8. To honor her Divine Maternity and her alliance with the Holy Trinity.
9. To honor her precious and loving death.
10. To honor her resurrection and triumphant Assumption.

May the grace of the Mystery of the Assumption come down into our souls. Amen.

5. The Coronation of the Blessed Virgin

We offer Thee, O Lord Jesus, this fifteenth decade in honor of the Coronation of Thy holy Mother; and we ask of Thee, through this Mystery and through her intercession, perseverance in grace and a crown of glory hereafter. Amen.

OUR FATHER. Glory of God: Inaccessible.

TEN HAIL MARYS.

1. To honor the triple crown with which the Holy Trinity crowned Mary.
2. To honor the new joy and glory that Heaven received by her triumph.
3. To confess her the Queen of Heaven and earth, of angels and of men.
4. To honor her as the treasurer and dispenser of God's graces, of the merits of Jesus Christ and of the gifts of the Holy Spirit.
5. To honor her as the mediatrix and advocate of men.
6. To honor her as the destroyer and ruin of the devil and of heresies.
7. To honor her as the sure refuge of sinners.
8. To honor her as the Mother and support of Christians.
9. To honor her as the joy and sweetness of the just.
10. To honor her as the universal refuge of the living and the all-powerful comfort of the afflicted, the dying and the souls in Purgatory.

May the grace of the Mystery of the Coronation of the Blessed Virgin come down into our souls. Amen.

THE FATIMA PRAYERS

Pardon Prayer

MY GOD, I believe, I adore, I hope, and I love Thee! I ask pardon for those who do not believe, do not adore, do not hope, and do not love Thee.

The Angel's Prayer

The children of Fatima prayed this prayer over and over, bowed low, with their foreheads touching the ground.

MOST Holy Trinity, Father, Son and Holy Ghost, I adore Thee profoundly. I offer Thee the Most Precious Body, Blood, Soul and Divinity of Jesus Christ, present in all the tabernacles of the world, in reparation for all the outrages, sacrileges and indifferences by which He Himself is offended. And through the infinite merits of His Most Sacred Heart and the Immaculate Heart of Mary, I beg of Thee the conversion of poor sinners.

Blessed Sacrament Prayer

MOST Holy Trinity, I adore Thee! My God, my God, I love Thee in the Most Blessed Sacrament!

O My Jesus

To be said after the Glory Be following each decade of the Rosary.

O MY JESUS, forgive us our sins, save us from the fires of Hell; lead all souls to Heaven, especially those who are most in need of Thy mercy.

Sacrifice Prayer

Our Lady of Fatima said to the children: "Sacrifice yourselves for sinners, and say many times, especially whenever you make some sacrifice":

O JESUS, I offer this for love of Thee, for the conversion of sinners, and in reparation for the sins committed against the Immaculate Heart of Mary.

WORDS OF OUR LADY OF FATIMA ON SAVING SOULS

"Pray! Pray a great deal, and make sacrifices for sinners, for many souls go to Hell because there is no one to pray and make sacrifices for them." (August 19, 1917).

WORDS OF OUR LADY OF FATIMA ON THE ROSARY

"Pray the Rosary every day, in order to obtain peace for the world and the end of the war." (May 13, 1917).

" . . . Continue praying the Rosary every day in honor of Our Lady of the Rosary, in order to obtain peace for the world and the end of the war, because only she can help you." (July 13, 1917).

"I am Our Lady of the Rosary. Continue to say the Rosary every day." (October 13, 1917).

THE 54-DAY ROSARY NOVENA

The 54-Day Rosary Novena consists of a Rosary (5-decade) prayed every day for 54 consecutive days. The Novena is based on the traditional 15 Mysteries of the Rosary. On the first 27 days of the Novena, the Rosary is prayed in Petition. On the remaining 27 days, the Rosary is prayed in Thanksgiving, whether or not one has received an answer to his Petition. In praying this novena, a person cycles through the Joyful, Sorrowful and Glorious Mysteries over and over.

To keep track, a person can mark out the letters J, S, G, J, S, G, etc. on 54 consecutive days of a calendar, then check off the appropriate letter after praying the Rosary on that day.

NOVENA TO
OUR LADY OF GOOD REMEDY

O QUEEN of Heaven and earth, most holy Virgin, we venerate thee. Thou art the beloved daughter of the Most High God, the chosen Mother of the Incarnate Word, the Immaculate Spouse of the Holy Spirit, the Sacred Vessel of the Most Holy Trinity. O Mother of the Divine Redeemer, who under the title of Our Lady of Good Remedy comes to the aid of all who call upon thee, extend thy maternal protection to us. We depend on thee, dear Mother, as helpless and needy children depend on a tender and caring mother.

Hail Mary . . .

O Lady of Good Remedy, source of unfailing help, grant that we may draw from thy treasury of graces in our time of need. Touch the hearts of sinners, that they may seek reconciliation and forgiveness. Bring comfort to the afflicted and the lonely; help the poor and the hopeless; aid the sick and the suffering. May they be healed in body and strengthened in spirit to endure their sufferings with patient resignation and Christian fortitude.

Hail Mary . . .

Dear Lady of Good Remedy, source of unfailing help, thy compassionate heart knows a remedy for every affliction and misery we encounter in life. Help me with thy prayers and intercession to find a remedy for my problems and needs, especially for *(Indicate your special intentions here)*. On my part, O loving Mother, I pledge myself to a more intensely Christian lifestyle, to a more careful observance of the laws of God, to be more conscientious in fulfilling the obligations of my state in life, and to strive to be a source of healing in this broken world of ours.

Dear Lady of Good Remedy, be ever present to me, and through thy intercession, may I enjoy health of body and peace of mind, and grow stronger in the faith and in the love of thy Son, Jesus.
Hail Mary . . .

V. Pray for us, O holy Mother of Good Remedy,
R. *That we may deepen our dedication to thy Son, and make the world alive with His Spirit.*

A CONSECRATION TO MARY

Hail Mary . . .

MY QUEEN, my Mother! I give myself entirely to you; and to show my devotion to you, I consecrate to you my eyes, my ears, my mouth, my heart, and my whole being. Wherefore, loving Mother, as I am your own, keep me, guard me, as your property and possession.

SWEET HEART OF MARY

SWEET Heart of Mary,
be my salvation.

MARY OUR MOTHER

From the Cross Our Lord looked down on His Mother
Mary and His beloved disciple St. John. Jesus said to Mary:
"Woman, behold thy son." Then He said to St.
John: "Behold thy mother."

"And from that hour, the disciple took her
to his own." (Cf. *John* 19:25-27).

LITANY OF OUR LADY

The Litany of Loreto
(For public or private use.)

Lord, have mercy on us.
   Christ, have mercy on us.
Lord have mercy on us. Christ, hear us.
   Christ, graciously hear us.
God the Father of Heaven,
   Have mercy on us.
God the Son, Redeemer of the world,
   Have mercy on us.
God the Holy Ghost,
   Have mercy on us.
Holy Trinity, One God,
   Have mercy on us.

Holy Mary, *pray for us.*
Holy Mother of God, *pray for us.*
Holy Virgin of virgins, *etc.*
Mother of Christ,
Mother of divine grace,
Mother most pure,
Mother most chaste,

Mother inviolate,
Mother undefiled,
Mother most amiable,
Mother most admirable,
Mother of good counsel,
Mother of our Creator,
Mother of our Saviour,
Virgin most prudent,
Virgin most venerable,
Virgin most renowned,
Virgin most powerful,
Virgin most merciful,
Virgin most faithful,
Mirror of Justice,
Seat of Wisdom,
Cause of our Joy,
Spiritual Vessel,
Vessel of Honor,
Singular Vessel of Devotion,
Mystical Rose,
Tower of David,
Tower of Ivory,
House of Gold,
Ark of the Covenant,
Gate of Heaven,
Morning Star,
Health of the Sick,
Refuge of Sinners,
Comforter of the Afflicted,
Help of Christians,
Queen of Angels,
Queen of Patriarchs,

Queen of Prophets,
Queen of Apostles,
Queen of Martyrs,
Queen of Confessors,
Queen of Virgins,
Queen of all Saints,
Queen conceived without Original Sin,
Queen assumed into Heaven,
Queen of the Most Holy Rosary,
Queen of Peace,

Lamb of God, Who takest away the sins of the world,
 Spare us, O Lord.
Lamb of God, Who takest away the sins of the world,
 Graciously hear us, O Lord.
Lamb of God, Who takest away the sins of the world,
 Have mercy on us.

V. Pray for us, O holy Mother of God,
R. *That we may be made worthy of the promises of Christ.*

Let Us Pray

Grant, we beseech Thee, O Lord God, that we Thy servants may enjoy perpetual health of mind and body, and by the glorious intercession of the Blessed Mary, ever Virgin, be delivered from present sorrow and enjoy everlasting happiness. Through Christ Our Lord. Amen.

THE MAGNIFICAT
(Words of Our Lady from Luke 1:46-55).

M Y SOUL doth magnify the Lord, and my spirit hath rejoiced in God my Saviour, because He hath regarded the humility of His handmaid: for

behold, from henceforth all generations shall call me blessed, because He that is mighty hath done great things to me, and holy is His Name. And His mercy is from genera-tion unto generations, to them that fear Him.

He hath showed might in His arm: He hath scattered the proud in the conceit of their heart. He hath put down the mighty from their seat, and hath exalted the humble. He hath filled the hungry with good things, and the rich He hath sent empty away. He hath received Israel His servant, being mindful of His mercy: as He spoke to our fathers, to Abraham and to his seed forever.

THE GREEN SCAPULAR PRAYER
By praying this aspiration we "water" a Green Scapular that we have given to, or "planted" near, someone who needs Our Lady's help for body or soul.

I MMACULATE Heart of Mary, pray for us now and at the hour of our death. Amen.

PRAYER TO
OUR LADY OF GUADALUPE

HOLY MARY of Guadalupe, Mystical Rose, intercede for Holy Church, protect the Sovereign Pontiff, help all those who invoke you in their necessities; and since you are the ever Virgin Mary and Mother of the True God, obtain for us from your most holy Son the grace of keeping our faith, sweet hope in the midst of the bitterness of life, burning charity, and the precious gift of final perseverance. Amen.

OUR LADY OF GUADALUPE
AND THE AMERICAS

Our Lady of Guadalupe was proclaimed "Patroness of Mexico" and "Empress of the Americas" by Pope Pius XII in 1945. In 1946 Pope Pius XII proclaimed her "Patroness of the Americas." In 1999 Pope John Paul II declared that December 12, the Feast of Our Lady of Guadalupe, would be a liturgical feast for the whole continent.

Our Lady of Guadalupe is also venerated as "Patroness of the Unborn."

THE PROTO-EVANGELIUM

"I will put enmities between thee and the woman, and thy seed and her seed: she shall crush thy head, and thou shalt lie in wait for her heel."   —*Genesis* 3:15

(Douay-Rheims Bible)

THE WOMAN CLOTHED
WITH THE SUN

"And a great sign appeared in heaven: A woman clothed with the sun, and the moon under her feet, and on her head a crown of twelve stars."—*Apocalypse* 12:1

PROCLAMATION OF THE DOGMA OF THE IMMACULATE CONCEPTION
From the Bull Ineffabilis Deus

" . . . By the authority of Our Lord Jesus Christ, by the authority of the blessed Apostles Peter and Paul, and by Our own authority, We declare, pronounce and define:

"The doctrine that maintains that the most Blessed Virgin Mary in the first instant of her conception, by a unique grace and privilege of the omnipotent God and in consideration of the merits of Christ Jesus the Saviour of the human race, was preserved free from all stain of Original Sin, is a doctrine revealed by God and therefore must be firmly and constantly held by all the faithful. . . ."

—Pope Pius IX
December 8, 1854

WORDS OF OUR LADY OF LOURDES TO ST. BERNADETTE (1859)

"I am the Immaculate Conception." "Pray for poor sinners!" "Penance!"

WORDS OF ST. BONAVENTURE

"The gates of Heaven will open to all who confide in the protection of Mary."

THE MIRACULOUS MEDAL
Revealed to St. Catherine Labouré in 1830

Our Lady's Immaculate Conception is portrayed by images that show her crushing the serpent's head under her foot—illustrating the fact that she was never under the power of Satan for one instant of her life, beginning at her very conception. Unlike the other children of Adam, her soul was always in the state of Sanctifying Grace and never bore the stain of Original Sin. We honor Our Lady's Immaculate Conception by wearing the Miraculous Medal and by praying the invocation inscribed upon it:

O Mary, Conceived without Sin

O MARY, conceived without sin, pray for us who have recourse to thee.

REJOICE, O VIRGIN MARY

REJOICE, O Virgin Mary, for thou alone hast destroyed all heresies in the whole world.

PRAYER TO
OUR LADY OF MT. CARMEL
(Never found to fail.)

O MOST beautiful Flower of Mt. Carmel, Fruitful Vine, Splendor of Heaven, Blessed Mother of the Son of God, Immaculate Virgin, assist me in this my necessity. *(Mention your intention.)* O Star of the Sea, help me and show me in this that thou art my Mother.

O holy Mary, Mother of God, Queen of Heaven and earth, I humbly beseech thee, from the bottom of my heart, to succour me in this necessity; there are none that can withstand thy power. Oh, show me in this that thou art my Mother!

O Mary, conceived without sin, pray for us who have recourse to thee. *(three times)*

Sweet Mother, I place this cause in thy hands. *(three times)*

(It is suggested to offer three times the Our Father, Hail Mary and Glory Be in thanksgiving.)

WORDS OF ST. JOHN BERCHMANS
Patron of Altar Servers

"If I love Mary, I am certain of perseverance and shall obtain whatever I wish from God."

PRAYER TO MARY,
MISTRESS OF THE ANGELS

Given by Mary to a Bernardine Sister in approximately 1937 and urged fervently by Our Lady to be printed and distributed.

O EXALTED QUEEN of Heaven, Sovereign Mistress of the Angels, thou who from the beginning hast received from God the power and the mission to crush the head of Satan, we humbly beseech thee to send down thy holy angels, that under thy command and by thy power, they may pursue the evil spirits, encounter them on every side, resist their bold attacks and drive them hence into the abyss of Hell.

"Who is like unto God?" "Holy Angels and Archangels, defend us and protect us!" "O kind and tender Mother, thou shalt ever remain our love and our hope." Amen.

SHORT CONSECRATION TO MARY
By St. Alphonsus Liguori

O HOLY MARY, my Mistress, into thy blessed trust and special keeping, into the bosom of thy tender mercy, I commend my soul and my body this day, every day of my life and at the hour of my death. To thee I entrust all my hopes and consolations, all my trials and miseries, my life and the end of my life, that through thy most holy intercession and thy merits, all my actions may be ordered and disposed according to thy will and that of thy Divine Son. Amen.

THE CHRISTMAS PRAYER

It is piously believed that whoever recites this prayer fifteen times a day from the Feast of St. Andrew (November 30) until Christmas will obtain what is asked.

HAIL AND BLESSED be the hour and the moment in which the Son of God was born of the most pure Virgin Mary at midnight, in Bethlehem, in piercing cold. In that hour vouchsafe, O my God, to hear my prayer and grant my desires, through the merits of our Saviour Jesus Christ and of His Blessed Mother. Amen.

NOVENA TO OUR LADY OF LOURDES

O EVER Immaculate Virgin, Mother of Mercy, Health of the Sick, Refuge of Sinners, Comfortress of the Afflicted, you know my wants, my troubles, my sufferings. Look upon me with mercy. When you appeared in the grotto of Lourdes you made it a privileged sanctuary where you dispense your favors, and where many sufferers have obtained the cure of their infirmities, both spiritual and corporal. I come, therefore, with unbounded confidence to implore your maternal intercession. My loving Mother, obtain my request. I will try to imitate your virtues so that I may one day share your company and bless you in eternity. Amen.

SALUTATION TO MARY
By St. John Eudes (17th century)

A copy of this prayer was found in a book belonging to St. Margaret Mary after her death. This salutation was zealously propagated by Father Paul of Moll, O.S.B. (Belgium), 1824-1896. He said: "This salutation is so beautiful! Recite it daily. From her throne in Heaven the Blessed Virgin will bless you, and you must make the Sign of the Cross. Yes! Yes! If only you could see—Our Lady blesses you. I know it!" "Offered for the conversion of a sinner it would be impossible not to be granted."

Hail Mary, Daughter of God the Father!

Hail Mary, Mother of God the Son!

Hail Mary, Spouse of God the Holy Ghost!

Hail Mary, Temple of the Most Blessed Trinity!

Hail Mary, Pure Lily of the Effulgent Trinity!

Hail Mary, Celestial Rose of the ineffable Love of God!

Hail Mary, Virgin pure and humble, of whom the King of Heaven willed to be born and with thy milk to be nourished!

Hail Mary, Virgin of Virgins!

Hail Mary, Queen of Martyrs, whose soul a sword transfixed!

Hail Mary, Lady most blessed, unto whom all power in Heaven and earth is given!

Hail Mary, My Queen and my Mother, My Life, my Sweetness and my Hope!

Hail Mary, Mother most amiable!

Hail Mary, Mother most admirable!

Hail Mary, Mother of Divine Love!

Hail Mary, IMMACULATE, conceived without sin!
Hail Mary, Full of grace, the Lord is with thee!
  Blessed art thou among women, and blessed is the
  Fruit of thy womb, JESUS!

Blessed be thy spouse, St. Joseph.
Blessed be thy father, St. Joachim.
Blessed be thy mother, St. Anne.
Blessed be thy guardian, St. John.
Blessed be thy holy angel, St. Gabriel.

Glory be to God the Father, who chose thee.
Glory be to God the Son, who loved thee.
Glory be to God the Holy Ghost, who espoused
  thee.
O Glorious Virgin Mary, may all men love and praise
  thee.
Holy Mary, Mother of God, pray for us and bless us,
  now, and at death, in the Name of JESUS, thy
  Divine Son! Amen.

WORDS OF ST. HILARY

"No matter how great a sinner one may have been, if he shows himself devout to Mary, he will never perish."

NOVENA PRAYER TO OUR MOTHER OF PERPETUAL HELP

O MOTHER of Perpetual Help, thou art the dispenser of all the gifts which God grants to us miserable sinners; and for this reason He has made thee so powerful, so rich and so bountiful, in order that thou mayest help us in our misery. Thou art the advocate of the most wretched and abandoned sinners who have recourse to thee. Come then to my aid, dearest Mother, for I recommend myself to thee. In thy hands I place my eternal salvation, and to thee do I entrust my soul. Count me among thy most devoted servants; take me under thy protection, and it is enough for me. For if thou wilt protect me, dear Mother, I fear nothing: not from my sins, because thou wilt obtain for me the pardon of them; nor from the devils, because thou art more powerful than all Hell together; nor even from Jesus, my Judge Himself, because by one prayer from thee, He will be appeased. But one thing I fear, that in the hour of temptation, I may neglect to call upon thee, and thus perish miserably.

Obtain for me, then, the pardon of my sins, love for Jesus, final perseverance, and the grace always to have recourse to thee, O Mother of Perpetual Help.

Hail Mary . . . (three times)

THE PROPHECY OF ISAIAS

"Behold a virgin shall conceive, and bear a son, and his name shall be called Emmanuel."   —*Isaias* 7:14

STABAT MATER

At the Cross her station keeping,
Stood the mournful Mother weeping,
   Close to Jesus to the last.

Through her heart, His sorrow sharing,
All His bitter anguish bearing,
   Now at length the sword had passed.

Oh, how sad and sore distressed
Was that Mother highly blest,
   Of the sole-begotten One!

Christ above in torment hangs;
She beneath beholds the pangs
   Of her dying, glorious Son.

Is there one who would not weep,
Whelmed in miseries so deep
   Christ's dear Mother to behold?

Can the human heart refrain
From partaking in her pain,
   In that Mother's pain untold?

Bruised, derided, cursed, defiled,
She beheld her tender Child
   All with bloody scourges rent.

For the sins of His own nation
Saw Him hang in desolation,
   Till His spirit forth He sent.

O thou Mother, Fount of love!
Touch my spirit from above,
    Make my heart with thine accord.

Make me feel as thou hast felt;
Make my soul to glow and melt
    With the love of Christ, my Lord.

Holy Mother! Pierce me through,
In my heart each wound renew
    Of my Saviour Crucified.

Let me share with thee His pain,
Who for all my sins was slain,
    Who for me in torments died.

Let me mingle tears with thee,
Mourning Him who mourned for me,
    All the days that I may live.

By the Cross with thee to stay,
There with thee to weep and pray,
    Is all I ask of thee to give.

Virgin of all virgins blest!
Listen to my fond request:
    Let me share thy grief divine.

Let me to my latest breath
In my body bear the death
    Of that dying Son of thine.

Wounded with His every wound,
Steep my soul till it hath swooned
   In His very blood away.

Be to me, O Virgin, nigh,
Lest in flames I burn and die,
   In His awful Judgment Day.

Christ, when Thou shalt call me hence,
Be Thy Mother my defense,
   Be Thy Cross my victory.

While my body here decays,
May my soul Thy goodness praise,
   Safe in Paradise with Thee. Amen.

SEVEN PRAYERS IN HONOR OF THE SEVEN SORROWS OF THE BLESSED VIRGIN MARY

Approved by Pope Pius VII in 1815.

Begin thus:

V. O God, come to my assistance.

R. *O Lord, make haste to help me.*

V. Glory be to the Father, and to the Son, and to the Holy Ghost,

R. *As it was in the beginning, is now, and ever shall be, world without end. Amen.*

(Continued . . .)

—First Sorrow—
The Prophecy of Simeon

I GRIEVE for thee, O Mary most sorrowful, in the affliction of thy tender heart at the prophecy of the holy and aged Simeon. Dear Mother, by thy heart so afflicted, obtain for me the virtue of humility and the gift of the holy Fear of God.

Hail Mary . . .

—Second Sorrow—
The Flight into Egypt

I GRIEVE for thee, O Mary most sorrowful, in the anguish of thy most affectionate heart during the flight into Egypt and thy sojourn there. Dear Mother, by thy heart so troubled, obtain for me the virtue of generosity, especially toward the poor, and the gift of Piety.

Hail Mary . . .

—Third Sorrow—
The Loss of the Child Jesus
in the Temple

I GRIEVE for thee, O Mary most sorrowful, in those anxieties which tried thy troubled heart at the loss of thy dear Jesus. Dear Mother, by thy heart so full of anguish, obtain for me the virtue of chastity and the gift of Knowledge.
Hail Mary . . .

—Fourth Sorrow—
Mary Meets Jesus
on the Way to Calvary

I GRIEVE for thee, O Mary most sorrowful, in the consternation of thy heart at meeting Jesus as He carried His cross. Dear Mother, by thy heart so troubled, obtain for me the virtue of patience and the gift of Fortitude.
Hail Mary . . .

—Fifth Sorrow—
Jesus Dies on the Cross

I GRIEVE for thee, O Mary most sorrowful, in the martyrdom which thy generous heart endured in standing near Jesus in His agony. Dear Mother, by thy afflicted heart, obtain for me the virtue of temperance and the gift of Counsel.

Hail Mary . . .

—Sixth Sorrow—
Mary Receives the Dead Body of Jesus in Her Arms

I GRIEVE for thee, O Mary most sorrowful, in the wounding of thy compassionate heart when the side of Jesus was struck by the lance and His heart was pierced before His body was removed from the cross. Dear Mother, by thy heart thus transfixed, obtain for me the virtue of fraternal charity and the gift of Understanding.

Hail Mary . . .

—Seventh Sorrow—
Jesus Is Placed in the Tomb

I GRIEVE for thee, O Mary most sorrowful, for the pangs that wrenched thy most loving heart at the burial of Jesus. Dear Mother, by thy heart sunk in the bitterness of desolation, obtain for me the virtue of diligence and the gift of Wisdom.

Hail Mary . . .

V. Pray for us, O Virgin most sorrowful,
R. *That we may be made worthy of the promises of Christ.*

Let Us Pray

Let intercession be made for us, we beseech Thee, O Lord Jesus Christ, now and at the hour of our death, before the throne of Thy mercy, by the Blessed Virgin Mary, Thy Mother, whose most holy soul was pierced by a sword of sorrow in the hour of Thy bitter Passion. Through Thee, O Jesus Christ, Saviour of the world, Who with the Father and the Holy Ghost live and reign world without end. Amen.

SEVEN PROMISES

According to St. Bridget of Sweden (1303-1373), the Blessed Virgin grants seven graces to those who honor her daily by saying seven Hail Marys while meditating on her tears and sorrows:

1. "I will grant peace to their families."

2. "They will be enlightened about the divine Mysteries."

3. "I will console them in their pains, and I will accompany them in their work."

4. "I will give them as much as they ask for, as long as it does not oppose the adorable Will of my Divine Son or the sanctification of their souls."

5. "I will defend them in their spiritual battles with the infernal enemy, and I will protect them at every instant of their lives."

6. "I will visibly help them at the moment of their death—they will see the face of their mother."

7. "I have obtained this grace from my Divine Son, that those who propagate this devotion to my tears and dolors will be taken directly from this earthly life to eternal happiness, since all their sins will be forgiven, and my Son will be their eternal consolation and joy."

A PRECIOUS OFFERING

St. John Vianney, the Curé of Ars, was accustomed in special necessities to offer to the Eternal Father, by the hands of Mary, our Divine Saviour all covered with blood and wounds. This, he said, was an infallible means to obtain the most precious graces. The following words may be used to make this offering:

O MARY, Mother of Sorrows, I beseech thee, by the inexpressible tortures thou didst endure at the death of thy Son, offer to the Eternal Father, in my stead, thy beloved Son all covered with blood and wounds, for the grace of *(make your request)*. Amen.

PRAYER TO OUR MOTHER OF SORROWS FOR A HAPPY DEATH

O MOTHER of Sorrows, by the anguish and love with which thou didst stand by the Cross of Jesus, stand by me in my last agony. To thy maternal heart I commend the last three hours of my life. Offer these hours to the Eternal Father in union with the agony of our dearest Lord. Offer frequently to the Eternal Father, in atonement for my sins, the Precious Blood of Jesus, mingled with thy tears on Calvary, to obtain for me the grace to receive Holy Communion with most perfect love and contrition before my death, and to breathe forth my soul in the actual presence of Jesus.

Dearest Mother, when the moment of my death has come, present me as thy child to Jesus; say to

Him on my behalf: "Son, forgive him, for he knew not what he did. Receive him this day into Thy kingdom." Amen.

REMEMBER, O VIRGIN MOTHER

REMEMBER, O Virgin Mother of God, when thou shalt stand before the face of the Lord, to speak favorable things in our behalf, that He may turn away His indignation from us.

BRIEF RENEWAL OF CONSECRATION TO JESUS THROUGH MARY

St. Louis De Montfort recommends the following brief act of consecration as a monthly or even daily renewal of the Consecration to Jesus through Mary for those who have made this Consecration—which is explained in his book entitled True Devotion to Mary.

I AM ALL THINE, and all that I have belongs to Thee, O my sweet Jesus, through Mary, Thy holy Mother.

O HEART MOST PURE

O HEART most pure of the Blessed Virgin Mary, obtain for me from Jesus a pure and humble heart.

HOW TO RECEIVE COMMUNION IN THE SPIRIT OF TRUE DEVOTION TO MARY

From True Devotion to Mary (nos. 270, 273), by St. Louis De Montfort

"After Holy Communion, inwardly recollected and holding your eyes shut, you will introduce Jesus into the heart of Mary. You will give Him to His Mother, who will receive Him lovingly, will place Him honorably, will adore Him profoundly, will love Him perfectly, will embrace Him closely, and will render to Him, in spirit and in truth, many homages which are unknown to us in our thick darkness. . . . There are an infinity of other thoughts which the Holy Ghost furnishes, and will furnish you, if you are thoroughly interior, mortified and faithful to this grand and sublime devotion which I have been teaching you. But always remember that the more you allow Mary to act in your Communion, the more Jesus will be glorified; and you will allow Mary to act for Jesus and Jesus to act in Mary in the measure that you humble yourself and listen to them in peace and in silence, without troubling yourself about seeing, tasting or feeling; for the just man lives throughout on faith, and particularly in Holy Communion, which is an action of faith: 'My just man liveth by faith.' (*Heb.* 10:38)."

THIRTY DAYS' PRAYER
TO THE BLESSED VIRGIN

EVER GLORIOUS and blessed Mary, Queen of Virgins, Mother of Mercy, hope and comfort of dejected and desolate souls! Through that sword of

sorrow which pierced thy tender heart whilst thine only Son, Christ Jesus Our Lord, suffered death and ignominy on the Cross; through that filial tenderness and pure love He had for thee, grieving at thy grief, whilst from His cross He commended thee to the care and protection of His beloved disciple St. John; take pity, I beseech thee, on my poverty and necessities; have compassion on my anxieties and cares; assist and comfort me in all my infirmities and miseries, of whatsoever kind.

Thou art the Mother of Mercies, the sweet Consolatrix and only refuge of the needy and the orphan, of the desolate and afflicted. Cast, therefore, an eye of pity on a miserable, forlorn child of Eve, and hear my prayer. For since, in just punishment of my sins, I find myself encompassed by a multitude of evils and oppressed with much anguish of spirit, whither can I fly for more secure shelter, O amiable Mother of my Lord and Saviour Jesus Christ, than under the wings of thy maternal protection? Attend, therefore, I beseech thee, with an ear of pity and compassion, to my humble and earnest request.

I ask it through the bowels of mercy of thy dear Son; through that love and condescension wherewith He embraced our nature when, in compliance with the Divine Will, thou gavest thy consent, and whom, after the expiration of nine months, thou didst bring forth from the chaste enclosure of thy womb to visit this world and bless it with His presence.

I ask it through that anguish of mind wherewith thy beloved Son, our dear Saviour, was overwhelmed on Mount Olivet when He besought His Eternal Father to remove from Him, if possible, the bitter chalice of His future Passion. I ask it through the threefold repetition of His prayers in the Garden, from whence afterwards, with dolorous steps and mournful tears, thou didst accompany Him to the doleful theatre of His death and sufferings. I ask it through the welts and sores of His virginal flesh occasioned by the cords and whips wherewith He was bound and scourged when stripped of His seamless garment, for which His executioners afterwards cast lots. I ask it through the scoffs and ignominies by which He was insulted; the false accusations and unjust sentence by which He was condemned to death, and which He bore with heavenly patience. I ask it through His bitter tears and bloody sweat, His silence and resignation, His sadness and grief of heart. I ask it through the blood which trickled from His royal and sacred Head when struck with the scepter of a reed and pierced with His crown of thorns.

I ask it through the excruciating torments He suffered when His hands and feet were fastened with gross nails to the tree of the Cross. I ask it through His vehement thirst and bitter potion of vinegar and gall. I ask it through His dereliction on the Cross when He exclaimed: "My God! My God! Why hast Thou forsaken me?" I ask it through His mercy extended to the Good Thief, and through His commending His precious soul and spirit into the hands of His Eternal Father before He expired, saying: "It is consummated." I ask it through the blood mixed with water which issued from His sacred side when pierced with a lance, and whence a flood of grace and mercy has flowed to us.

I ask it through His immaculate life, bitter Passion and ignominious death on the Cross, at which nature itself was thrown into convulsions by the bursting of rocks, rending of the veil of the Temple, the earthquake, and darkness of the sun and moon. I ask it through His descent into hell, where He comforted the Saints of the Old Law with His presence and led captivity captive.

I ask it through His glorious victory over death, when He arose again to life on the third day; and through the joy which His appearance for 40 days after gave thee, His Blessed Mother, His Apostles, and the rest of His disciples, when in thine and their presence He miraculously ascended into Heaven. I ask it through the grace of the Holy Ghost infused into the hearts of His disciples when He descended upon them in the form of fiery tongues, and by which they were inspired with zeal for the conversion of the world when they went forth to preach the Gospel.

I ask it through the awful appearance of thy Son at the last dreadful day, when He shall come to judge the living and the dead, and the world by fire. I ask it through the compassion He bore thee in this life, and the ineffable joy thou didst feel at thine Assumption into Heaven, where thou art eternally absorbed in the sweet contemplation of His divine perfections. O glorious and ever blessed Virgin! Comfort the heart of thy supplicant, by obtaining for me *(here mention or reflect on your lawful request, under the reservation of its being agreeable to the will of God, who sees whether it will contribute toward your spiritual good)*.

And as I am persuaded that my Divine Saviour doth honor thee as His beloved Mother, to whom He refuses nothing, because thou askest nothing contrary to His honor, so let me speedily experience the efficacy of thy powerful intercession, according to the tenderness of thy maternal affection and His filial loving heart, who mercifully granteth the requests and complieth with the desires of those that love and fear Him. Wherefore, O most blessed Virgin, besides the object of my present petition, and whatever else I may stand in need of, obtain for me also of thy dear Son, Our Lord and our God, a lively faith, firm hope, perfect charity, true contrition of heart, unfeigned tears of compunction, sincere confession, worthy satisfaction, abstinence from sin, love of God and my neighbor, contempt of the world, patience to suffer affronts and ignominies, nay, even, if necessary, an opprobrious death itself, for love of thy Son, our Saviour Jesus Christ.

Obtain likewise for me, O sacred Mother of God, perseverance in good works, performance of good resolutions, mortification of self will, a pious conversation through life, and, at my last moments, strong and sincere repentance, accompanied by such a lively and attentive presence of mind as may enable me to receive the Last Sacraments of the Church worthily and die in thy friendship and favor.

Lastly, obtain through thy Son, I beseech thee, for the souls of my parents, brethren, relatives and benefactors, both living and dead, life everlasting, from the only Giver of every good and perfect gift, the Lord God Almighty: to whom be all power, now and forever. Amen.

THE END OF OUR LADY'S LIFE

The Church teaches that at the end of her earthly life, the Blessed Virgin was assumed, body and soul, to the glory of Heaven. Although the Church has not decided the question of whether Our Lady actually died before her Assumption, it is generally held that she did die. This would have been fitting, as she would thus have followed the pattern of her Son's life.

In 1892 Our Lady's house was rediscovered in Ephesus, Turkey. Today it is a site of pilgrimage.

THE ROSARY IN LATIN

*The asterisk in some prayers shows where the
response begins when the Rosary is prayed
aloud by a group of persons.*

Symbolum Apostolorum
The Apostles' Creed

CREDO in Deum Patrem omnipotentem, Creatorem caeli et terrae; et in Jesum Christum, Filium eius unicum, Dominum nostrum, qui conceptus est de Spiritu Sancto, natus ex Maria Virgine, passus sub Pontio Pilato, crucifixus, mortuus, et sepultus: descendit ad infernos, tertia die resurrexit a mortuis, ascendit ad caelos, sedet ad dexteram Dei Patris omnipotentis, inde venturus est judicare vivos et mortuos. *Credo in Spiritum Sanctum, sanctam Ecclesiam catholicam, sanctorum communionem, remissionem peccatorum, carnis resurrectionem et vitam aeternam. Amen.

Pater Noster
Our Father

PATER NOSTER, qui es in caelis, sanctificetur nomen tuum. Adveniat regnum tuum. Fiat voluntas tua sicut in caelo et in terra. *Panem nostrum quotidianum da nobis hodie; et dimitte nobis debita nostra, sicut et nos dimittimus debitoribus nostris. Et ne nos inducas in tentationem. Sed libera nos a malo. Amen.

Ave Maria
Hail Mary

AVE MARIA, gratia plena: Dominus tecum: bene-
dicta tu in mulieribus, et benedictus fructus
ventris tui, Jesus. *Sancta Maria, Mater Dei, ora pro
nobis peccatoribus, nunc et in hora mortis nostrae.
Amen.

Gloria Patri
Glory Be

GLORIA PATRI, et Filio, et Spiritui Sancto.
*Sicut erat in principio, et nunc et semper, et in
saecula saeculorum. Amen.

O Mi Jesu
O My Jesus

O MI JESU, dimitte nobis debita nostra, salva nos
ab igne inferni, perduc in caelum omnes ani-
mas, praesertim eas, quae misericordiae tuae maxime
indigent.

Salve Regina
Hail Holy Queen

SALVE REGINA! Mater Misericordiae, vita, dul-
cedo, et spes nostra, salve! Ad te clamamus,
exsules filii Evae. Ad te suspiramus, gementes et
flentes in hac lacrimarum valle. Eia ergo, advocata

nostra, illos tuos misericordes oculos ad nos con-
verte. Et Jesum, benedictum fructum ventris tui,
nobis post hoc exsilium ostende. O clemens, O pia,
O dulcis Virgo Maria!

V. Ora pro nobis, sancta Dei Genitrix,
R. *Ut digni efficiamur promissionibus Christi.*

ACT OF TOTAL CONSECRATION TO JESUS THROUGH MARY

These two paragraphs are the heart of the 8-paragraph Act of Total Consecration to Jesus through Mary as taught by St. Louis De Montfort. This Act is not simply a prayer; it is a commitment. The Act of Total Consecration is usually made after a preparation of 30 days as explained in the book True Devotion to Mary, by St. Louis De Montfort. The Act begins by addressing Jesus, but the following two paragraphs are addressed to Mary Immaculate.

I, (Name), a faithless sinner, renew and ratify today in thy hands the vows of my Baptism; I renounce forever Satan, his pomps and works; and I give myself entirely to Jesus Christ, the Incarnate Wisdom, to carry my cross after Him all the days of my life, and to be more faithful to Him than I have ever been before.

In the presence of all the heavenly court I choose thee this day for my Mother and Mistress. I deliver and consecrate to thee, as thy slave, my body and soul, my goods, both interior and exterior, and even the value of all my good actions, past, present and future; leaving to thee the entire and full right of disposing of me, and all that belongs to me, without exception, according to thy good pleasure, for the greater glory of God, in time and in eternity.

MY MOTHER, MY CONFIDENCE!
Mater Mea, Fiducia Mea!

O MARY Immaculate, the precious name of Mother of Confidence, with which we honor thee, fills our hearts to overflowing with the sweetest consolation and moves us to hope for every blessing from thee. If such a title has been given to thee, it is a sure sign that no one has recourse to thee in vain. Accept, therefore, with a mother's love, our devout homage, as we earnestly beseech thee to be gracious unto us in our every need. Above all do we pray thee to make us live in constant union with thee and thy Divine Son, Jesus. With thee as our guide, we are certain that we shall ever walk in the right way, in such wise that it will be our happy lot to hear thee say on the last day of our life those words of comfort: "Come then, my good and faithful servant; enter thou into the joy of thy Lord." Amen.

My Mother, my Confidence!